One Act Plays That Have Nothing to do With Each Other

Written by Drake Dalgleish

Cover Art Photographed by: Madeline Cooper

Table of Contents

The Guy on My Roof

Written by
Drake Dalgleish

Genre:
Comedy

Length:
7 - 10 minutes

Characters:
Guy (m)
Mary (f)

Setting:
Outside Mary's house. Night. Present day.

Description:
When Mary wakes up at 3 in the morning to see a stranger sitting on her roof, she is not happy! Mary insists that he leaves at once but he refuses because "He's stuck on the view." It's a quick funny show with a pretty good lesson about how everything changes so you should enjoy the little things while you can.

The Guy on My Roof:

Lights Up on GUY, sitting on the roof of Mary's house. There is a ladder on the side of the house. He sits there smiling with his feet dangling. It's a peaceful night. He takes a deep breath of air, taking in the view and everything around him. He starts to whistle a nice soft tune. MARY enters from her front door trying to find out where the whistling is coming from. GUY doesn't notice her as he's still taking in the view and whistling. She eventually sees him and screams.

GUY: Howdy!

MARY: *(Panicked and Confused)* What are you doing on my roof?

GUY: Oh you know, just enjoying the view.

MARY: On MY roof?

GUY: Yup!

MARY pauses in confusion.

MARY: Why can't you do this on your own roof?

GUY: Because I don't have one. Well, actually I do. Just not with a view like this.

MARY: Then go find another roof! You're on my property.

GUY: I've already tried all the other roofs on this block, and this one has the best view.

MARY: Of what?

GUY: Everything! The moon, the stars, the city, and all the other houses. It's beautiful.

MARY: I will call the police if you do not get off my roof right now!

GUY: Why?

MARY: Because you are causing a disturbance!

GUY: Actually, I think you'll find you're the one here causing a disturbance.

MARY: What?

GUY: Well, you see, I'm just trying to sit here and enjoy the view, while you're screaming away at... *(Checks watch)* 3AM. People are trying to sleep.

MARY: But I can't sleep when there's a stranger sitting on the roof of my house!

GUY: Why not?

MARY: Because, you're trespassing on my property! I want you off my roof now!

GUY: Sorry. No can do.

MARY: Why not?

GUY: I'm stuck.

MARY: No you're not, I can see the ladder you used to get up here.

GUY: Not on the roof. I'm stuck on this view. It's just so breath taking.

MARY: Who are you?

GUY: *(Thinks)* I don't know.

MARY: You don't know your name?

GUY: No, I know my name. I just don't know who I am right now. Who I am and who I want to be. Still trying to figure that out.

MARY: Ugh! Forget it. I don't even want to know your name. What I want is for you to get off my roof!

GUY: Already told you, can't do that.

MARY: And I already told you, I don't care. Get off my roof Now!

GUY: *(Shrugs)* Sorry.

MARY: Fine! Then I'll just have to force you off myself.

MARY makes her way over to the ladder, but before she can start to climb it, GUY kicks the ladder over. MARY get's even more irritated.

MARY: You son of a-

GUY: Woah there, no need to be swearing.

MARY sets ladder back up, but GUY kicks it back down. MARY just looks at GUY.

GUY: Even though I'd prefer not to, I could do this all night. Can you just let me enjoy the view?

MARY: I told you, I can't sleep with a stranger sitting on my roof!

GUY: Okay. Well, how about you watch the view with me then.

MARY: What? I'm not gonna sit on the roof with you.

GUY: Have you even looked at this view?

MARY: I don't care about some stupid view of the moon, stars, city, any of it! If I wanted to look at that stuff I'd just google it, instead of doing something stupid like sitting on the roof at three in the morning!

GUY: Wow, your wonder must have died a long time ago.

MARY: What?

GUY: Instead of experiencing a breath taking view in real life, you'd rather look it up and look at a picture on a computer.

MARY: Whatever.

GUYS goes back to watching the view and whistling softly his sweet tune.

MARY: Can you just please do me a favor and get off my roof? I'm tired and I need to sleep.

GUY: Do you need sleep, or do you just want to go to sleep?

MARY: Both!

GUY: Well go to bed then. Why argue with a guy who is clearly determined to watch this view, when you can just go inside lay in your nice warm bed and sleep. And when you wake up in the morning I won't be here.

MARY: Well what about you? Don't you need sleep?

GUY: Need sleep? Yes. But do I want to? No.

MARY: Why?

GUY: Someone like you wouldn't understand.

MARY: Someone like me?

GUY: Someone with no wonder left in the world. Someone who doesn't appreciate the little things in life, like this beautiful view.

MARY: I don't need my life to be criticized by a guy who's sitting on my roof. I also don't Want it!

GUY: Well, you may not want to be criticized, but you are gonna want to see this view.

MARY: I told you I don't care about the view.

GUY: Well what do you care about?

MARY: Getting you off my roof.

GUY: Such a shame, no one else will get to see it.

MARY: Then take a picture.

GUY: Again, no wonder. A picture is nothing like the the real thing. Sure you can be where ever you are, lets say an office. You can pull out your phone or look on your computer and pull up a picture of it and saying "Huh that's pretty neat!" but it is nothing like experiencing it with your own eyes. Actually being there. It's a feeling like no other. Just come on up here and you'll understand.

MARY: I'm not gonna climb up on my roof.

GUY: Oh come on!

MARY: Can't I just see it from down here?

GUY: Nope you got too many fences, trees, and a Big O'l pole in the way. You gotta come up here to see it.

MARY thinks to herself. She tries to look at the view from where she is. Then she looks at the ladder. Then she looks at GUY who waves at her.

MARY: Alright, I'll make you a deal. I'll come up there for three minutes, but after three minutes you get off my roof and leave.

GUY: *(Thinks about the offer)* Okay, you got yourself a deal. But don't you even think of pushing me off this roof!

MARY: Relax, I won't.

MARY crosses over to the ladder. She picks it up and leans it on the house. She then climbs up the ladder. After getting up to the roof she carefully makes her way to the center where GUY is sitting.

MARY: *(Looking at GUY)* Alright now, where is this view you were talking about?

*GUY points out towards the audience *Note: he is not pointing at the audience members, just out into the house.* MARY is suddenly blown away by the view.*

MARY: Oh my god. This is..... Beautiful.

GUY: That's one word for it.

MARY: Wow.

GUY: That's two! *(Pause)* Now I have a question for you. Do you still need sleep?

MARY: Yes.

GUY: Do you want to sleep?

MARY: *(Pause)* No. No I don't.

GUY: Now you get it.

MARY: Gosh I could just sit here all night and never get board of what I'm looking at.

GUY: Well you probably should.

MARY: *(Still stuck on the view)* Why?

GUY: Because nothing lasts forever.

MARY is sucked out of the moment and looks at GUY.

GUY: Our world is built on change. People are always trying to come up with things to out shine the things we already have and replace them. Records to MP3's, Books to Movies, ect. ect. Some people are aware that if they want to get rich they need to Keep making new things, so they build things that aren't meant to last so they can build a better version later. Like your car, your phone, your computer. Even this city is subject to change. New buildings are being built, old buildings being torn down. And it changes what you're looking at for better or for worse. Even simple structures being built can ruin a view. *(Beat)* See that big pole right there. Tomorrow, they're putting up a build board right there. Gonna cover up the whole view. Once it's up it'll be gone forever. That's why I'm up here on your roof. To get one last look at one of the greatest views I've ever seen. I'm glad I was able to share it with someone else.

They look back at the view. GUY'S watch beeps, it's been three minutes. Breaks them out of the moment again.

GUY: Well it's been three minutes, a deals a deal.

MARY: Wait, you don't have go. If you love this view why don't you stay till it's gone? Enjoy it as much as you can.

GUY: Probably cause it will hurt to see it go away. Plus it's as I said earlier. Our world is built on change. As one view is destroyed, another can be created. Since this one will be gone soon, I gotta go find that next view. Plus I've had a long enough time with this one. I'll let you have the rest of it.

GUY gets up.

MARY: Wait, I still have no idea who you are.

GUY: I told you already. I still don't know who I am either. I'm still trying to figure that out. Huh, maybe I'm just a guy who goes around finding new views to look at. And maybe even sharing them with a stranger.

MARY: *(Awkwardly)* I meant what's your name.

GUY: *(Embarrassed)* Oh right! Sorry. My name's Guy.

MARY: I'm Mary. It was nice talking to you Guy.

GUY: You too.

GUY gets down from the roof by crawling down the side of the house. He exits.

MARY: *(Shouting to GUY offstage)* Wait you left your ladder!

GUY: *(Offstage)* Actually that's not even my ladder, It was just siting there. Hell, I didn't even use it to get up on the roof.

MARY sits on the roof looking out at the view with a happy smile on her face. Lights Fade to Black.

THE END

Production notes: The Guy on My Roof

If you don't have the budget to build a fake house, feel free to get creative with the set. As long there is a hight difference, it should be fine.

The Room

Written by
Drake Dalgleish

Genre:
Horror / Thriller

Length:
5 - 10 minutes

Characters:
Jamie (m/f)
Zombies / Whispers (m/f)
Reporter (f)
Cops 1 & 2 (m/f)
Chief (M)

Setting:
Jamie's bedroom.

Description:
Jamie comes home in a panic, after "the end of the world" has begun. Now trapped in the room, alone and afraid. Can Jamie make it through the night locked in the room? This is a new stage horror / thriller experience that while very quick, is sure to send a chill up your spine.

Scene 1:

Lights up on a bedroom. *The walls are dark blue, with movie posters all around them. Stage Left there is a door with a lock on it. The door opens into the room. Next to the door is light switch that is on the wall above a big dresser. Against the wall Center Stage is a small desk with a chair. The desk has an old lamp resting at the end of it. There is a clock hanging above the desk. On the wall Stage Right is a window white trimming around it. It has dark blue blinds that are closed so you cannot see through it. There is also a tv next to it. The tv screen is facing the audience. There is a twin bed on the wall next to the window. Around the room there are also empty pill bottles, but they should not stand out much. They should be subtle.* The clock ticks in the empty room for a bit. Suddenly the door bursts open, and JAMIE storms in and shuts the door quick behinds him and leans on it. JAMIE looks around panicked. He sees the dresser to his left. He quickly pushes it in front of the bedroom door. He steps away from the door. He watches the door. Silence, nothing but the ticking of the clock. He sighs in relief. Suddenly there is a thunderous ponding on his door. JAMIE screams and backs up. Along with the pounding there are moans of zombies outside.

JAMIE: Shit! Shit! Shit!

The pounding and moaning continues as JAMIE curls into a ball by the desk. After a bit, the ponding stops. The moans stay for a bit, but they fade away. JAMIE notices.

JAMIE: Thank God.

JAMIE gets up. He thinks for a moment. He decides to turn on the tv. There is a news report. THE REPORTER, very panicked and is driven to the point of tears, is still able to make this announcement.

REPORTER: The end is here. The dead have risen and are roaming the streets of the city. We have no confirmed reports of this being a world wide epidemic, or what the militaries plans are on dealing with this crises. I urge you all to stay inside your homes, lock the doors. Just be safe. *(Beat)* Amy, Zoe. If you are watching this, mommy loves you so much an-

Suddenly we hear a door burst open and zombie moans. THE REPORTER looks away from the camera and screams. The news feed cuts out. It is now the emergency broadcast screen. JAMIE turns off the tv.

JAMIE: No, no, no. This can't be happening!

JAMIE checks his phone to try and make a call.

JAMIE: No signal.

Moans are heard outside the door again. Jamie is quiet. The moaning fades. JAMIE goes to his desk. He looks through his drawers. He first pulls out a pistol, a small revolver, and sets it on the desk. He then pulls out a notebook and a pencil. He sits in his chair and starts to write. As he writes, he speaks.

JAMIE: So this is it. This is how it all ends. Probably would have preferred a solar flare wiping us all out, or a massive flood. *(Pause)* I've barricaded the door, and my window should be okay since I live on the 4th floor. I think my biggest problem will be starvation and dehydration if I stay here to long. *(Looks up at the clock)* It's currently midnight. If I try to leave now, I'd be lost in the dark and I'd probably get eaten. I'm going to wait till morning to leave. It's safer that way. If someone is reading this and I did not make it out of this room alive, if it's not to much, please bury my body by that tree outside the apartment. I've always enjoyed watching and listening to the birds in that tree.

He puts down the pen and closes the note book. He leaves it on the desk and walks over to his bed. He lays on the bed and tries to sleep. Just as JAMIE closes his, there is a tapping on his window. His eyes are wide open. He slowly gets up as the tapping continues. His hands shake as he grabs onto the string of the blinds. He pulls down on the string quick and the blinds fly open to reveal nothing. JAMIE starts to calm down. Suddenly there a is a flash through the window. Thunder and Lightning. JAMIE screams as there is a blackout. JAMIE fumbles around in the dark. He finally finds the lamp on the desk and turns it on. The lights are now up, just dimmer than before. Lightning strikes again. JAMIE goes over to the window and closes the blinds.

JAMIE: It's just a little lightning. Nothing to be scared of.

Suddenly the moans start to fade back in. They come closer to the room. The pounding on the door starts again, this time there are more of them. JAMIE backs up bumps into the lamp on his desk. The lamp falls over and breaks. Blackout. He pulls out his phone to use the flashlight. He points it at his face. He's Hyperventilating. He points it at the door. The pounding is more violent. He puts down the phone with the flashlight facing up. JAMIE rocks back and forth holding himself and crying. The pounding continues to get more and more violent. JAMIE is at a breaking point.

JAMIE: *(Bursting out)* STOOOOOP!

Silence. The pounding has stopped, and the moans are gone. JAMIE, breathing heavily, looks at the door. Then he looks out to the audience. The battery on his phone dies causing the flashlight to turn off. Blackout. Lights up as dark blue to represent the darkness of the room. JAMIE sits on the floor in the dark. No sound at all except the ticking clock. JAMIE sees he cut himself on the chards of the lamp. He goes to his bed and tears off some of the sheet and wraps it around the wound. He sits on the bed.

WHISPER 1: Jamie…

JAMIE becomes fearful, looking around trying to see where that noise came from.

WHISPER 2: Jamie…

JAMIE: Who said that?

WHISPER 1: Open the door...

WHISPER 2: Open the door, Jamie...

WHISPER 3: Let us in...

JAMIE looks at the door.

JAMIE: What?

WHISPER 2: Open the door, Jamie...

WHISPER 3: Let us in...

WHISPER 1: Don't be afraid...

JAMIE stands up and towards the door and stops himself by the desk.

JAMIE: This can't possible be real. I'm just going crazy.

WHISPER 1: We're real Jamie...

WHISPER 2: You can trust us...

WHISPER 3: Open the door...

JAMIE: No, no. My mind is just playing tricks on me. It's just voices. Don't listen.

WHISPER 1: You can't Ignore us, Jamie...

WHISPER 2: Open the door...

WHISPER 3: We just want to help you…

WHISPER 1: We know you're afraid…

WHISPER 2: Very afraid…

WHISPER 3: We can help you, Jamie…

WHISPER 1: Just open the door…

WHISPER 2: Let us in…

WHISPER 3: You don't have to sit alone…

WHISPER 1: In the dark…

WHISPER 2: We can help you…

JAMIE: Help me how?!

WHISPER 3: Just let us in, Jamie…

JAMIE: Just shut up! You're not real. This is all just in my head.

Violent pounding hits the door. It scares JAMIE.

WHISPER 1: We're real, Jamie…

WHISPER 2: Open the door…

WHISPER 3: Let us in…

JAMIE: No.

Pounding becomes more violent.

WHISPER 1: Open the door…

WHISPER 2: Let us help you…

WHISPER 3: Open up…

JAMIE: Leave me alone!

WHISPER 1: Not until you open the door, Jamie…

WHISPER 2: We won't leave until this door opens…

WHISPER 3: Let us in…

JAMIE: Shut Up!!

JAMIE curls into a ball on the floor, covering his ears, as the pounding grows louder and louder along with the whispers. The Whispers start to overlap with each other, saying things like "Jamie" "Open the door" "Let us in". JAMIE screams and stands up. He can't take it anymore. He picks up the pistol he left on his desk.

JAMIE: Fine!

JAMIE storms over to the door and pushes the dresser out of the way.

JAMIE: You want me to open the door. I'll open it!

JAMIE swings open the door and light shines through. All lights go out except the one coming from the door. He points the gun out the door. He shoots once.

COP 1: Shit!

COP 2: Drop him!

JAMIE is shot a multitude of times until he finally hits the ground. Two cops come in with flashlights on and looks at the body of JAMIE. COP 1 picks up JAMIE's gun and COP 2 checks for a pulse.

COP 2: Dead.

Blackout.

Scene 2:

Lights up on JAMIE's room. The door has yellow caution tape around it. JAMIE's body is under a blood covered blanket. The two cops stand around talking to each other. CHIEF comes into the room.

COP 1: Chief!

CHIEF: What the hell happened here?

COP 2: Sir, we were just-

CHIEF: I don't want excuses! I want to know what happened.

COP 1: Well sir, we got a call of a noise complaint from one of Jamie Cooper's neighbors, saying there was screaming and banging on the wall. So we came to check it out.

COP 2: When we got here, we knocked on his door. We asked him to let us in, told him we were just here to help, but he said we weren't real.

COP 1: Eventually he opened the door, but he had a gun and he shot at us.

COP 2: I was taken by surprise and... I made the call the open fire. Before we could get a grasp of what was happening, it was too late.

COP 1: After that we searched the place. He had written what looked like a suicide note in his journal. There was blood on the ground next to shards of a broken lamp and we found a few empty pill bottles that were prescribed to Jamie Cooper.

COP 2: We're sorry boss. We didn't know the whole situation. We thought he was dangerous or insane. We made a mistake.

CHIEF: We'll talk about this more later. Get out of here.

COP 1 & 2: Yes, sir.

COP 1 & 2 exit. CHIEF looks around the crime scene a bit.

Fade to Black.

THE END

Production notes: The Room

Jamie is written as a male character, but please feel free to gender bend this role.

If you don't have a lot of actors, double casting is an option. I would recommend having the cops and the chief be the zombies and whispers.

For the whispers, you can try to have them whisper from behind the door, but I would recommend having a surround sound system to have the voices bounce around the performance space. Adds to the eeriness.

Feel free to change any explicit language to something more appropriate, if needed.

The Boys

Written by
Drake Dalgleish

Genre:
Comedy

Length:
12 - 17 minutes

Characters:
Derek (m)
Chase (m)
Dan (m)
Steven (m)
Jeremy (m)
Gavin (m)

Setting:
Living room
Car
A yard

Description:
You think you have a weird and crazy group of friends, get a load of the boys! Derek is here to tell you about his crazy friends and a few experiences they've shared together. This comedy is all about sticking with your old friends, even if they can drive you a little crazy.

Scene 1:

Lights Up on a living room. It has a small couch and tiny coffee table in front of it. From offstage we hear screams. Suddenly all the boys come in with nerf swords It's a gigantic battle, people getting hit left and right. Some of them getting more wailed than others. STEVEN grabs a nerf bow and starts shooting everyone. The boys gang up on STEVEN. As they tackle him to the floor they freeze. DEREK walks out of the pile up and goes to the side.

DEREK: You're probably wondering "What the hell did I just walk into?", and I honestly can't tell you. I have no clue what's going on. That pretty much sums up every time I hang out with theses guys. Hi, I'm Derek, and these guys right here are my friends. *(Looks as them)* Well some of my friends. I have more friends than just these guys, but they are my friends. They're my pretty good friends. I like to refer to them as The Boys. Because even though we're all about 18, we are no where close to being adults. Example A *(Gestures to the fight)* There will be plenty more examples where that came from.

Blackout on the boys as they exit.

DEREK: So where to start? I guess I should introduce them.

They all walk out in a line and wave to the audience. Spot on CHASE.

DEREK: This is Chase. He's the most athletic one of our group, and really loves competition. I knew him first out of the group and we've always been close.

Spot on DAN.

DEREK: This is Dan. He's also one of the more athletic ones. He can be pretty chill at times, but he can go from 0 to 100 real quick if he's really into something.

Spot on STEVEN

DEREK: This is Steven. He's the smartest of the group, and he loves to cause mischief in anyway he can when playing games.

Spot on JEREMY.

DEREK: This is Jeremy. He's kind of smart. Like he knows a lot of things, but he makes a lot of stupid choices.

Spot on GAVIN.

DEREK: And then there's Gavin. Don't get me wrong I love him, but he's not the smartest. I'll leave at that. *(To them)* Thanks guys.

The boys leave.

DEREK: Those are the boys. We've been friends since elementary school, and we've done a lot together. They come over to my house a lot. My place is just the spot to hang out I guess. They do text me when they come over, sometimes. Other times they'll come over at the most random time with the weirdest things.

Scene 2:

A door bell rings. DEREK walks over to the door and opens it. It's STEVEN and JEREMY holding steaks.

STEVEN: Hey.

JEREMY: We brought steaks. Can we use your grill?

DEREK: It's almost midnight.

STEVEN: Yeah, perfect time to cook.

They come in and walk off stage. Door bell rings again. DEREK opens the door and it's CHASE and DAN holding soccer balls.

CHASE: Dude let's go kick penalties at the school.

DAN: And on the ways we can stop at Taco Bell.

DEREK: There's no lighting at the field and It's almost dark, how will we see the ball coming at us?

DAN: That's the challenge!

CHASE: First I gotta use your bathroom.

CHASE and DAN come into the house and exit. The door bell rings yet again. DEREK opens the door to see GAVIN with his phone out.

GAVIN: Wanna play some Pokemon Go?

DEREK: Gavin, we have an hour before school starts.

GAVIN: Yeah! So no one is gonna be at the lake, we can take over the gyms!

DEREK: *(Thinks)* Alright just give me a minute. Wanna come in?

GAVIN comes in the house and exits. Lights down spot on DEREK.

DEREK: Example B. It doesn't end there though. Sometimes I'll be busy all day with work or something, and when I come home late at night-

GAVIN & CHASE: GOOOOAAAAALLLL!

Lights Up on the living room. The boys are playing video games.

DEREK: They'll be there. *(Crossing over to them.)* What are you guys doing here?

JEREMY: We wanted to hang out.

DEREK: Okay, but how'd you get in?

STEVEN: You're mom let us in.

GAVIN: And she made us dinner.

DEREK: Of course she did. *(Back to audience.)* And then we will stay up all night either doing something crazy like walking around at 3 in the morning or playing games till we all hate each other. A lot of the time, we end up playing monopoly for 5 hours, which ends in Steven always screwing us over.

Lights down on the scene as the boys exit. Spot on DEREK.

DEREK: They're there, even when I'm not. My point is, they basically live at my house. I'm sure everyone has a friend or two like that. Well I have a whole group of them. So yeah my friends drive me a little crazy sometimes and sometimes I join in on the madness.

Scene 3:

Lights Up on the sword fight again. They're back in their frozen position. DEREK makes his way back to his spot.

DEREK: Back to Example A.

The boys unfreeze and it's a frenzy of swords hitting bodies again. Steven shoots past DEREK with the nerf bow.

DEREK: Steven, watch where you aim!

CHASE holds JEREMY in a head lock and point his JEREMY's butt towards STEVEN.

CHASE: Steven, get him in the ass!

Everyone freezes.

DEREK: As I said, weird. Don't judge us. It's 4 in the morning.

Unfreeze. STEVEN aims again and hits JEREMY right in the butt. JEREMY screams while laughing and falls over holding his butt. Everyone else starts laughing as the sword fighting continues. DAN and GAVIN break from the group and have there own sword fight. DAN is practically beating the crap out of GAVIN.

GAVIN: Dude, not so hard! Derek, Help.

DEREK runs over and starts to fight DAN with GAVIN. STEVEN aims bow at DEREK. He shoots and misses and hits a lamp off stage. Lamp breaks. Everyone stops.

DEREK: Steven, I told you to watch where you're aiming!

STEVEN: Sorry, I was aiming for you, but you moved.

DEREK: You always break something.

JEREMY: How about we move the fight to the back yard, so we don't break anything else.

DAN: Sounds Good.

The boys exit as DEREK stays.

DEREK: Wait Steven. Get back here! You have to clean this up! *(To audience)* Then I end up picking up the mess. There not as bad as you may think though. Plus I've known them since like first grade, we grew up together. And I mean, madness can be fun sometimes.

Lights Down and spot on DEREK.

Scene 4:

DEREK: There was a period of time where my house would get hit with all sorts of pranks. From people leaving wooden logs, raisins, and roadsigns at my door step. And you know those sticks you use for shish kebab's? Someone stuck my yard with a hundred of those suckers. I picked them up and put them a trash bin. So one day we we're hanging out at my house, and I told them about it and suddenly Jeremy said.

Lights Up on the boys in the living room.

JEREMY: Let's go pranking!

DEREK: And to my surprise, everyone was on board.

DAN: Yes, let's do it!

GAVIN: I'm in!

CHASE: I'll drive!

STEVEN: Derek, you in?

DEREK: Well who would we prank? We can't just hit anyone.

CHASE: He's right. We need to plan this out. A multitude of houses!

JEREMY: Where are the sticks?

DEREK: In a box in the trash bin outside.

JEREMY: Gavin, let's get them!

JEREMY and GAVIN exit.

STEVEN: So where are we gonna hit?

CHASE: Gavin just got our of a relationship right? Let's ask him it we can prank her house.

DAN: Perfect! *(Shouting to GAVIN)* Hey Gavin!

GAVIN: *(Offstage)* What?

DAN: What's your ex's name again?

GAVIN: *(Offstage)* Britney?

DAN: Yeah, do you know where she lives?

GAVIN: *(Offstage)* Yeah, why?

CHASE: How about we prank her house?

GAVIN: *(Offstage)* Dude Yes!

STEVEN: Alright, we have a target. Derek, are you in?

DEREK: *(Thinks)* You know what? Yeah, okay. Let's do it!

Everyone cheers. STEVEN, CHASE, and DAN exit. Spot on DEREK.

Scene 5:

DEREK: Normally, I'd just say no and we'd play monopoly like we always do. But something in me said screw it. Do something different, something crazy. So I got in the car.

Lights Up on the boys in a car. CHASE is in the drivers seat and JEREMY is in the back behind the seats. DEREK crosses over to the car.

DEREK: Originally I was sitting in the middle back, but for narration purposes I'll be taking shot gun. So we left for the house. She lived up in the hills, but Gavin forgot to tell us-

GAVIN: So she lives on a really long private drive.

CHASE: What?

DEREK: Which was a problem because-

CHASE: Dude it's the midnight of the night.

STEVEN: They'll see the headlights coming a mile away.

JEREMY: Why did't you tell us this before we drove out here.

GAVIN: Sorry it slipped my mind.

DAN: God Damnit, Gavin.

DEREK: So what do we do?

They think.

CHASE: Screw it.

CHASE turns off the headlights. Blackout. Everyone starts freaking out.

DEREK: He turned off the headlights and started driving down the road slowly. We couldn't see anything. I was scared he was gonna drive us right off the road. *(Actors do what is said here)* So we roll down the windows and we all turn on our phones and use the light of our screen to see the edges of the narrow road. And somehow we made it to the house undetected. Chase put the car into get away position and turned on the lights inside the car.

Lights Up on them inside the car.

JEREMY: So you guys ready for this?

STEVEN: Who wants to get out of the car?

GAVIN: Well for sure I'm going.

CHASE: I'm staying here, get away driver's got to be ready.

JEREMY: Dan, Steven, Derek?

STEVEN: We shouldn't all get out, if we get caught, we can't take the time to all pile in.

DAN: I'm with Steven on this one.

DEREK: I'll do it.

JEREMY: And I will too. Alright. Let's go.

JEREMY and GAVIN exit the car.

DEREK: And so I go too.

Blackout.

Scene 6:

Lights Up on DEREK, JEREMY, and GAVIN crawling from Stage Right on the lawn with sticks in there hands.

JEREMY: *(Whispering)* Nice and easy. Don't make to much noise.

DEREK: For some reason I think, "This is gonna go great!" everything looks fine. Until-

GAVIN stands up and starts putting sticks in the ground rapidly.

DEREK: *(Whispering)* GAVIN!

JEREMY: *(Whispering)* What are you doing!?

GAVIN: Relax, it doesn't look like anyone's home. Either that or they're asleep. We're in the clear.

GAVIN runs off towards the house, Stage Left.

DEREK: Wait!

JEREMY: You know maybe he's right. It looks like nobody's here. I think we'll be okay.

DEREK: *(To audience)* He legitimately said this.

JEREMY: Dude this is gonna be a walk in the park.

DEREK: *(To audience)* You see where this is going right?

Suddenly a light comes from off Stage Left. With a shadow of a person holding a rake.

DEREK: *(Whispering)* Shit, the garage door is opening.

JEREMY: *(Whispering)* Jesus!

DEREK: *(Whispering)* Stay down. Maybe he won't see us.

JEREMY: *(Whispering)* Wait, where's Gavin?

Suddenly GAVIN screams. DEREK and JEREMY get up and run off Stage Right.

DEREK: Oh Crap!

JEREMY: Back to the car!

Blackout.

Scene 7

Lights up on the car, CHASE is starting up the engine.

STEVEN: Crap they've been spotted!

DAN: Get the car ready!

CHASE: I am!

DEREK and JEREMY dive into the car.

STEVEN: Where's Gavin?

GAVIN dives in the car.

GAVIN: Go he's right behind me. Go!

CHASE: Hang on!

DEREK: *(What he narrates happens)* Chase turns on the headlights, hits the gas and takes off. But the guy is still chasing us on foot!

JEREMY: He's right behind us!

STEVEN: Go Faster!

CHASE: I'm trying!

DEREK: We slowly speed up, but the guy is full on sprinting behind us, right on our tail.

Mass screams of panic from everyone in the back.

DEREK: Finally we start to leave him in the dust, but we're now going almost 40 on the narrow road. *(To CHASE)* Hey we've almost lost him. You can slow down.

CHASE: No! Not until we're out of the driveway!

DEREK: We're gonna crash if you don't slow down!

CHASE: Just let me drive!

DEREK: *(To audience)* He speeds up even more! My heart is beating out of my chest. When finally we get to the end of the driveway an on the main road.

Everyone cheers. After cheers it's filled with a bit of silence.

CHASE: So... who's up for taco bell?

Everyone cheers again!

DEREK: We did it.

Blackout.

Scene 8:

Lights Up on the living room everyone is eating and laughing. DEREK stands up.

DEREK: So after that, we went through the taco bell drive through, Gavin bought us all soft tacos, and we came back to my place to "lay low". It was a crazy night which ended with us playing monopoly again. *(Crosses Down Stage)* This is probably one of my favorite memories with these guys, because I don't think I would have done this with anyone else. Hell, I don't think I would have done it unless these guys told me to. You see, I'm telling you this story, because I know everyone has those crazy friends in there life who on a daily basis make you question "Why am I still friends with these idiots?" Well this is exactly why. While sometimes they'll do things that just irritate the shit out of you, they also get you to do things you would never do in a million years. They bring out my crazy side, make you feel alive and I need that. Everyone needs to act crazy once in a while. I spend most of my time trying to meet up to peoples standards, but with the boys I can just let go and be freakin weird all I want. So hold on to your crazy friends, cause they give you the most out of life. *(Beat)* Well I hope you enjoyed, but I gotta go now. After a bit or sword fighting, tonights gonna be the night we beat Steven at Monopoly! Hopefully.

Fade to Black.

THE END

Production notes: The Boys

Feel free to change any explicit language to something more appropriate, if needed.

For the Car scenes, you can either use car seats or use rehearsal boxes to represent a car.

During the "Car Chase" scene, I would recommend driving sound effects to increase tension.

Royalty Information

As stated in the title, these one acts have nothing to do with each other. These are all separate shows, they just all live in the same script. If you wish to do a scene or a monologue from any these plays for any sort of competition like The International Thespian Society I.E. events, that is perfectly okay. Just be sure to reach out to the author first.

You cannot perform these shows without obtaining the royalties first. Any performances without consent from the author is a violation of copyright law and you will be punished. If you wish to perform any of the short plays in this book, or other plays written by Drake Dalgleish, you must buy the royalties. You can do so by contacting the author by emailing DrakeAllenDalgleishPlays@gmail.com

There you can talk with Drake Dalgleish about what plays you would like to perform, the price of the royalties, and other information you need.

ISBN-10: 1545569576

ISBN-13: 978-1545569573

Authors Note

Thank you so much for reading *One Act Plays That Have Nothing to do With Each Other.*

After publishing my first play, *Lonely Windows,* I knew I wanted to get back to writing right away, but I couldn't think of a solid story idea. Then one night, while I was laying in bed an idea came to me. I pulled out my laptop and typing away putting whatever came to mind on the page. Eventually that story became *The Guy on My Roof.* After it was finished I tried to publish it by itself, but through amazons self publish I was not able to because the page count was too low. I had no clue what I was going to do. Then one day I was in my local theatre reading a script that was in a collections book and it hit me.

So for 4 months, I started brainstorming ideas for other short one act plays to write. When an Idea came I wrote it down and hammered it out. I came up with 7 ideas, but only 3 of them got finished. Not every idea you have is gonna work, but when you find the ones that do it can be incredible. I enjoyed writing all the short stories in this collection and when I get the inspiration I'll probably get started on another collection.

I really hope you enjoyed these short stories. Until next time.

Drake Allen Dalgleish
6/6/2017

Acknowledgments

Susan Donahue
Madeline Cooper
Sparrow Lynn
Delany Morgan
Jeremy Snyder
Mikiah Salinas
Quinn Anderson
Kaleb Anagnostou
Evan Hennessey
Nolan Abell
Ian Ward
Jeri & Duane Dalgleish
Sadie Dalgleish
Tuddie & Melvin Macie
Hunter Bell
Josh Adell

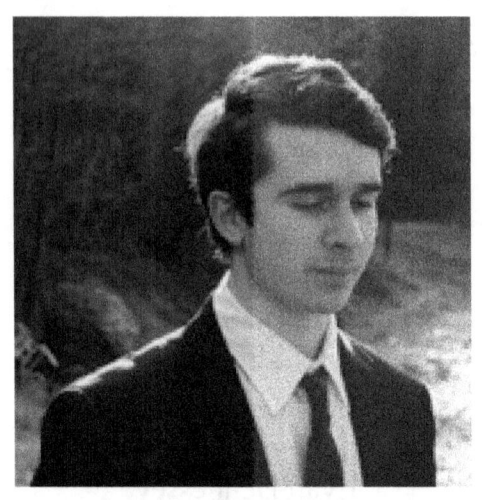

About the Author
Drake Allen Dalgleish:
(18 years old as of 2/2/17)

Actor, Singer, Writer, Director, and Film Editor. Drake does it all. He has been involved in over 30 theatre productions since his freshman year of high school in 2013. He helped write 7 of those productions. This is Drake's second time publishing and he feels proud of all the stories in this book and he hopes you enjoyed reading these stories as much as he enjoyed writing them.

To keep up with Drake's current projects, check out his Facebook page: https://www.facebook.com/DrakeDalgleishActor

www.ingramcontent.com/pod-product-compliance
Lightning Source LLC
Chambersburg PA
CBHW061224180526
45170CB00003B/1154